EXTREME NATURE

DEEP SEA
EXTREMES

NATALIE HYDE

Crabtree Publishing Company
www.crabtreebooks.com

Crabtree Publishing Company
www.crabtreebooks.com

Author: Natalie Hyde

Editor: Molly Aloian

Proofreaders: Adrianna Morganelli, Katherine Berti

Project coordinator: Robert Walker

Production coordinator: Margaret Amy Salter

Prepress technician: Samara Parent

Project editor: Tom Jackson

Designer: Lynne Lennon

Picture researchers: Sophie Mortimer, Sean Hannaway

Managing editor: Tim Harris

Art director: Jeni Child

Design manager: David Poole

Editorial director: Lindsey Lowe

Children's publisher: Anne O'Daly

Photographs:
Corbis: Tobias Bernhard: page 6 (top); Roger Ressmeyer:
    page 6 (bottom); Amos Nachoum: page 7 (top); Rick Price:
    page 10 (bottom); Denis Scott: page 14 (left); Handout:
    pages 17 (top), 20; Lynda Richardson: page 17 (bottom);
    Stephen Frink: page 18 (top); Jeffrey L. Rotman: page 19 (top);
    Ralph White: page 23 (top); Tim Rue: page 23 (bottom);
    Bettmann: page 29 (top)
NASA: page 27; GSFC: pages 4-5; HSF: pages 24-25
NaturePL: David Hall: front cover; David Shale: pages 8 (bottom),
    12-13, 16; Florian Graner: page 19 (bottom); Doug Allan:
    page 21 (bottom)
NOAA: J. Morin: pages 8-9; David Burdick: page 9 (right);
    P. Rona: page 10 (top); Dr. Steve Ross: page 11 (top);
    M. Youngbluth: page 13 (top); Bruce Moravchik: page 15 (top);
    Steve Nicklas: page 23 (center)
Photoshot: A.N.T. Photo Library: pages 14-15
Science Photo Library: Paul Zahl: page 13 (bottom);
    Christian Darkin: page 18 (bottom); Bill Bachman:
    page 29 (bottom)
Shutterstock: Vera Bogaerts: page 7 (bottom); Tatyana Morozova:
    page 28
U.S. Navy: page 4; Christopher Perez: page 24; H. Wolfgang Porter:
    page 25

Illustrations:
Darren Awuah: page 5
BRG: pages 22-23, 26, 27

Every effort has been made to trace the owners of copyrighted material.

Library and Archives Canada Cataloguing in Publication
Hyde, Natalie, 1963-
    Deep sea extremes / Natalie Hyde.

(Extreme nature)
Includes index.
ISBN 978-0-7787-4501-3 (bound).--ISBN 978-0-7787-4518-1 (pbk.)

    1. Deep-sea ecology--Juvenile literature. 2. Deep-sea animals--
Juvenile literature. I. Title. II. Series: Extreme nature (St. Catharines,
Ont.)

QH541.5.D35H93 2008   j577.7'9   C2008-907341-X

Library of Congress Cataloging-in-Publication Data

Hyde, Natalie, 1963-
    Deep sea extremes / Natalie Hyde.
        p. cm. -- (Extreme nature)
    Includes index.
    ISBN 978-0-7787-4518-1 (pbk. : alk. paper) -- ISBN 978-0-7787-4501-3
(reinforced library binding : alk. paper)
    1. Deep-sea ecology--Juvenile literature. 2. Deep-sea animals--Juvenile
literature. I. Title. II. Series.

QH541.5.D35H94 2008
578.77'9--dc22
                                                    2008048639

Crabtree Publishing Company
www.crabtreebooks.com   1-800-387-7650

Published in Canada
Crabtree Publishing
616 Welland Ave.
St. Catharines, Ontario
L2M 5V6

Published in the United States
Crabtree Publishing
PMB16A
350 Fifth Ave., Suite 3308
New York, NY 10118

CONTENTS

INTKODUCTIUN

If you looked at Earth from outer space, you would see that most of it is covered by water. Almost three-quarters of the planet's surface is sea. The waters are divided into five regions: the Pacific, Atlantic, Indian, Arctic, and Southern Oceans.

ON THE FLOOR

The ocean floor is not flat. There are mountain ranges, deep valleys, and huge plains. Near the coast, oceans are shallow with flat seabeds. The flat area is called the continental shelf.

HOW DEEP IS IT?

Long ago, sailors measured the depth of the sea using a rope holding a weight. The rope was marked into fathoms, lengths of 6 feet (1.8 m). As it was lowered over the side, a sailor counted the marks until the weight touched the seabed. Today, scientists use a beam of sound to make a picture of a seabed (*left*). Computers measure how long it takes for the sound to echo off the seabed. Scientists can then figure out how far down it is.

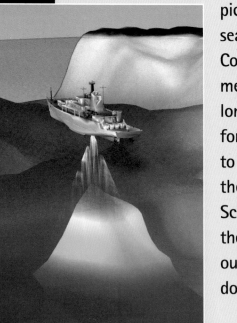

Challenger Deep is the deepest seabed on Earth. It is located in the Mariana Trench in the Pacific Ocean. The seabed is 35,838 feet (10,923 m) below the surface of the water. If Mount Everest was in the trench, its peak would be one mile (1,609 m) under water!

◄ *Earth looks mainly blue from space because of all the water on its surface. No other planet has liquid water on its surface.*

1. sunlight zone — 1
650 feet (198 m)

2. twilight zone — 2
0.6 miles (one km)

3. midnight zone — 3

2.4 miles (four km)

4. abyssal zone — 4

+3.7 miles (+ 6 km)

5. ocean trench — 5

INTO THE DEEP

The continental shelf reaches about 40 miles (65 km) from shore. Then, the shelf slopes down steeply to the deep ocean floor. This area is called the **abyssal** plain. The very deepest parts of the oceans are trenches that plunge down thousands of feet into the plain. Most undersea earthquakes and **volcanic eruptions** happen near these trenches.

◄ *The deeper you go in the oceans, the darker the water gets. Below about 2.4 miles (four km) there is never any light at all.*

IN THE DARK

It is a very different world at the bottom of an ocean. Daylight can reach only about 650 feet (198 m) into the water. Below that, it becomes as dark as night. Deeper than 2.4 miles (four km), it is pitch black all the time. Plants cannot live where there is no light, but some animals have adapted to survive on the ocean floor.

FAST FACTS

★ The Southern Ocean near Antarctica is the coldest. In some places, the water is 28.5 °F (−1.9 °C).

★ The highest temperatures are found near underwater volcanoes (*right*). There, the water is 660 °F (350 °C)!

★ Cusk eels have been found at five miles (8.4 km) below the surface.

UNDER PRESSURE

The pressure in the deep sea is very high. The pressure at sea level is measured as one atmosphere (one atm). If you climb a mountain, the pressure goes down because there is less air pushing down from above. Water is heavier than air, so pressure increases very quickly as you travel deeper. Every 32 feet (10 m) of water above you adds one atm to the pressure. Deep divers wear hard suits (*left*) to stop their bodies being crushed by the pressure. Even a naval submarine would be smashed by the pressure below 2,400 feet (731 m).

COLD AND HEAVY

Water never freezes on the ocean floor. One reason for this is because it is salt water. Saltwater freezes at a colder temperature than **freshwater**—about 28 °F (-2 °C). Water this cold is less **dense** than warmer water, so it floats to the surface. Even in the Arctic Ocean— where the surface of the ocean is frozen for most of the year—the water at the bottom of the sea never gets cold enough to form ice.

▲ *Ice is less dense than water. As a result, it floats at the surface forming huge icebergs, leaving warmer water near the ocean floor.*

LIFE WITHOUT LIGHT

Plants cannot live in the deepest parts of the oceans. They can only grow where there is light. Deep-sea creatures must find other types of food.

In the Extreme

Amphipods (*below*) look like little fleas but are relatives of shrimps. They live deeper than almost any other animals. There is little food in this deep habitat. Amphipods eat marine snow if they can find it. Sometimes, they act like tiny piranhas and rip flesh off dead animals.

FALLING FOOD

Most deep-sea animals eat snow—**marine snow**. Marine snow is made up of the leftover bits of plants and animals from near the surface. The pieces stick together as they sink, making them look like flakes of snow. This "snow" sinks slowly to the seabed. It can take weeks to reach the bottom, where it forms a blanket of ooze on the seabed.

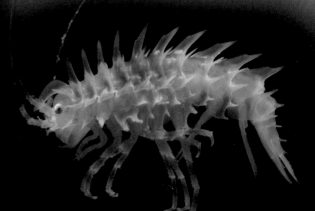

GO WITH THE FLOW

All the oceans are connected by a slow-moving flow of water called the thermohaline current. Cold, salty water is heavier than warm, less-salty water. The heavy, cold water sinks near the poles. Then it starts flowing over the abyssal plain. It pushes warmer water back toward the poles. This current spreads the **nutrients** from marine snow to all corners of the sea floor.

SIMPLE RELATIONS

Tunicates (*below*) are animals that look like plants. They rest on the seabed and pump water through their tube-shaped bodies to sieve out any marine snow. It is thought that all **vertebrates** evolved from something similar to a tunicate. A tunicate can rebuild its body after an injury. Scientists are investigating whether the same system could one day be used to heal injured humans!

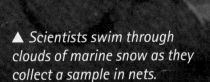

▲ *Scientists swim through clouds of marine snow as they collect a sample in nets.*

CHEMICAL DINNER

The ocean floor has cracks in it where water can trickle into the rocks of the seabed. Some of these cracks are near undersea volcanoes. The water in the rocks is heated by **magma**, and the super-hot water is pushed back up into the ocean through cracks called **hydrothermal vents**. This hot water is full of **dissolved minerals**. Some of the minerals form into solid lumps around these vents. Gradually, the crystals build up and make tall chimneys.

▶ *When the warm water inside a vent mixes with the cold water of the deep sea, the chemicals in it form a thick, dark cloud. Vents like this are called black smokers.*

LITTLE HELPERS

The water around hydrothermal vents is poisonous. It is hard to believe anything can survive here, but some animals do. Tubeworms have no mouth or stomach. They use a feathery plume (*right*) to collect chemicals from the water. However, the worm cannot live on these chemicals. **Bacteria** living inside the tubeworm's body changes the chemicals into useful nutrients. This process of making food is called chemosynthesis.

▲ *Most of the deep ocean has few living things, but hydrothermal vents are full of life. The first vents were discovered in 1977 when scientists began to explore the seabed with submarines.*

CHILLED FOOD

Sometimes, the water that comes up through the ocean floor is not heated. However, it still contains many chemicals. These places are known as cold seeps. Mounds of ice form around cold seeps. However, the ice is not made from water, but **methane**. Scientists have discovered that animals survive even here. Ice worms burrow into the methane to get away from giant isopods—a huge type of deep-sea pill bug!

Vital Statistics

✶ Despite their name, ice worms have a pair of legs for crawling and swimming.

✶ The worms live around cold seeps. They make burrows in the methane ice.

✶ Scientists believe that the worms feed on bacteria that live on the surface of the ice.

ANIMAL LIFE

In a world of total darkness far away from sunlight, animals in the deep sea have found a way to make their own light. Light produced by living things is called bioluminscence. The light is made by body **cells** called photophores. Photophores use chemicals to produce a range of different colors.

GLOW IN THE DARK

Bioluminescence may be used to scare off predators or to attract mates. Every type of light-producing animal has a unique pattern of lights. The red jewel squid has photophores that cover its entire body. They make it look like a giant strawberry!

▼ As well as making it twinkle in the darkness, an anglerfish can also wiggle the "fishing rod" on its head to attract prey.

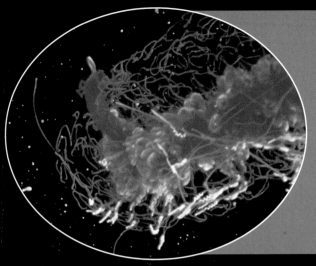

STINGING JELLY

Siphonophores look like long jelly ropes. Some grow to 130 feet (40 m). They catch fish in their tentacles using stinger cells. The siphonophores also twinkle with red bioluminescence. Most animals produce blue or green light. The siphonophore is one of the few that create red light.

FISHING FOR FOOD

Anything that glows looks like something to eat. The anglerfish uses light to catch food. It has a spine poking out of the top of its head. The tip of the spine hangs above the fish's huge mouth. Photophores on the tip flash on and off to lure smaller fish into its mouth.

Vital Statistics

* Lantern fish have photophores all along their sides but two are located right below their eyes.

* The fish (*left*) is nicknamed the Headlight Fish for the light coming from its head.

* Lantern fish can make blue, green, or yellow lights.

LIVING WITH PRESSURE

The pressure at the bottom of the oceans would flatten a human's body. Why are ocean-dwellers not squeezed to death by the weight of all the water above them? They stay in one piece because the pressure inside their bodies is equal to the pressure on the outside. However, deep-sea animals cannot survive at the surface. The high pressure inside makes their bodies explode!

In the Extreme

Sperm whales (*below*) swim deeper than any other **mammal**. They swim down two miles (3.2 km). The whale has a flexible rib cage that allows its lungs to shrink as they are squeezed by the water pressure. The heart also slows because it is very difficult for it to pump blood around the body. Even without a good supply of blood, the muscles keep working. They are able to store **oxygen** before a dive.

UNDER GLASS

Glass sponges live in the deepest parts of the oceans. They use silica, the same mineral humans use to make glass, to build an amazingly strong skeleton (*left*). The skeleton can withstand the huge pressure on the ocean floor. Scientists are studying glass sponges to figure out how they make glass at low temperatures and how to make better **optical fibers.**

◀ *Sea cucumbers live in all areas of the ocean floor. They look for food in the mud.*

KEEPING ON MOVING

Animals in the deep sea still need to swim or walk through the high-pressure water. Sea cucumbers do not have shells or bones. Their bodies are filled with liquid. This is pumped around the body to make it move and change shape—in the same way **hydraulic** pistons control a crane.

STAYING AFLOAT

Most fish use a gas bag, called a swim bladder, to control how they float. Filling the bladder with gas makes the fish float up. Releasing the gas makes the fish sink.

▲ *Fanfin sea devils are relatives of anglerfish.*

FINDING THE WAY

Animals that live in total darkness have had to come up with new ways to find food and mates. Without any light to see, they rely on other senses. For example, the fanfin sea devil is a deep-sea hunter. Its strange name matches the way it looks. Its fleshy body is covered with long spikes. These spikes work like a cat's whiskers to pick up the slightest movements in the water. The sea devil sits motionless until another fish swims past. The hunter can pinpoint the position of this prey by feeling the currents it makes as it swims through the water.

In the Extreme

The tripod fish has three long fins that look like legs. Even though the fish's body is 14 inches (36 cm) long, its fins can be more than three feet (one m)! Most of the time the tripod fish stands on its three fins on the bottom of the ocean. The fish faces into the current, waiting for prey to drift by. The fish senses objects in the water with its front fins. The fins act like hands. Once they feel prey, the fins knock the food into the fish's mouth.

FAST FACTS

✳ Most fish that live in the dark have huge eyes with wide **pupils**. This helps them capture every tiny bit of light that comes from animals nearby.

✳ The bony snout of a goblin shark (*below*) is filled with electricity sensors. The shark scans the seabed in the dark to locate fish by the tiny electric currents made by their muscles.

SOUND SYSTEM

Bottlenose whales dive almost as deep as sperm whales. Like other whales, they use echolocation to find their way around in the dark. The whale produces loud clicks and chirping sounds. These sounds bounce off objects, and the whale listens to the echoes to find food such as fish and squid.

▼ *Freshwater eels spend most of their lives in rivers, but adults swim out to sea to breed on the sea floor. The eels in the Atlantic Ocean gather in the depths of the Sargasso Sea northeast of the Caribean.*

GETTING PROTECTION

Sea creatures work hard to stay away from **predators**. Because there are not many places to hide on the abyssal plain, creatures have found ways to disappear. The black medusa jelly has almost perfect **camouflage**. Like many animals in the deep, this jellyfish is see-through. However, it is also covered with a velvety, black umbrella that absorbs all the light that hits it. It is so good at being invisible that it was not discovered until 1992.

▼ *Gulper eels live below 6,562 feet (2,000 m) underwater. They can grow to about 5 feet (1.5 m) long and have mouths that are wide and stretchy enough to swallow animals that are almost as large as the eels themselves!*

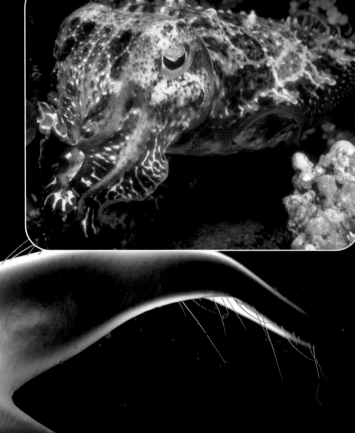

LAST LINE OF DEFENSE

Sea cucumbers cannot move very fast. They have had to develop other ways to protect themselves. When in danger, a sea cucumber will turn its stomach inside out—and it shoots out of its body. This will frighten away the predator. The sea cucumber does not die. It grows a new stomach in a few weeks.

IT'S A STICK UP

The deep-sea spanish dancer is a sea slug. It does not lose its insides when in danger—it loses its outside instead! When attacked, the slug's skin lights up and sticks to the attacker. A predator wearing this bright, sticky mask might become dinner himself!

▶ *A spanish dancer is named for the frills along its side that look like the skirts worn by women in Spain.*

FAST FACTS

⭐ Sea stars can survive losing an arm when they are attacked. Just like lizards on land, which can grow new tails, sea stars can grow new arms.

⭐ Deep-sea animals that are not transparent, or see-through, are usually black or red. In the darkness, red looks black so both are good colors for staying hidden.

▼ *This fish only looks red because a flashlight is shining on it. The color of the fish depends on the color of the light shining on it.*

GIGANTIC CREATURES

There is not a lot of food in the deep ocean. One way of surviving in such places is to grow to a huge size. Big bodies are much more efficient than smaller ones. Large animals need to eat larger meals but they need to eat less often. Their bodies also generate more heat, which helps in cold water, and they use less oxygen.

▼ *This colossal squid is the largest ever found. It was hauled up from the deep sea around Antarctica and weighed more than half a ton (495 kg)!*

TALL STORIES

For centuries sailors told stories about giant sea creatures that had huge eyes and tentacles longer than their ships. Were these tales true?

▲ Stories about giant squid often described them as being much larger and more dangerous than they really are.

REAL MONSTERS

In 1925, two enormous tentacles were found in the stomach of a sperm whale. They belonged to one of the largest deep-sea animals of all—the giant squid. The giant squid grows to 60 feet (18 m) long! It takes a long time to grow to this size. The biggest squids might be more than 50 years old. The colossal squid is not as long but is much heavier, making it the largest **invertebrate** in the world.

Vital Statistics

* The giant isopod is one of the few animals living on the deep ocean floor that has a hard shell.

* It is a relative of the pill bugs and wood lice that live in damp places on land.

* The giant isopod (*below*) can grow to 14 inches (35 cm) long.

* Its shell is made up of separate plates, which make it flexible as well as strong.

THE HUMAN EXPERIENCE

It may surprise you to learn that we know more about the surface of other planets than we do about our own ocean floor. The cold, pressure, and darkness make exploration to the deepest parts very difficult.

▼ The crew of Trieste were amazed to see fish living even in the deepest ocean.

hatch

gasoline tank

DIVE DIVE!

In 1957, *Trieste* was the first craft to reach Challenger Deep, the deepest place on Earth. The crew sat in a ball-shaped cabin underneath a large float. The float was full of gasoline and had **ballast** tanks of water and iron pellets. The ballast made the craft sink slowly. It took almost five hours to reach the bottom. To get home, the crew dropped the ballast. The gasoline left in the float was lighter than water, and so *Trieste* began to rise to the surface.

window

iron ballast

DEEP EXPLORER

The *Alvin* was one of the first HOVs, or Human Occupied Vehicles, to explore the deep ocean floor. It can carry a pilot and two passengers. It has its own lights, a robotic arm, and a basket for collecting samples. *Alvin*'s crew found the first hydrothermal vents, and the sub also explored the wreckage of the *Titanic*.

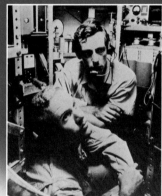

▶ *Jacques Piccard (top) and Don Walsh are the only people to have dived to Challenger Deep.*

FAST FACTS

✶ Rescue submarines have a dome that fits over the hatch of any other submarine. Sailors can climb from one ship to the other without having to swim in cold, deep water.

✶ An ROV is a Robot Operated Vehicle. Without a human crew, an ROV can stay under water for days. The human operator stays on the surface and can see where the ROV is using a camera (left).

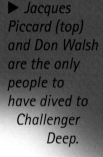

light

23

BENEATH THE WAVES

A modern naval submarine can stay under water for as long as it needs to. The conditions for the crew inside are the same as on land—the sub makes air and freshwater from the seawater outside and has enough fuel to keep going for years. The crew only has to come to the surface to load more food.

LIVING UNDER THE SEA

Divers swimming in deep water cannot stay down for long. Also, they cannot swim back to the surface quickly. The rapid change in pressure could kill them. If a diver is hurt, he or she cannot rush to hospital. Astronauts have the same problems in space. NASA uses an undersea training center called Aquarius to practice living in space. Aquarius has bedrooms, a bathroom, and a kitchen. Outside, there is a gazebo with an air pocket inside. Here, divers can take off their masks and chat.

▶ *Divers pose for a holiday photo inside and out of the Jules Verne diving lodge 21 feet (6.4 m) below the waters of the Florida Keys.*

COUNTDOWN

When people stay under water, the pressure causes nitrogen gas to collect in their blood. If they stay too long or come to the surface too quickly, the nitrogen forms bubbles in the blood. The bubbles block the blood vessels and can kill or cause brain damage. This is called the bends because the pain makes people squirm in agony.

In the Extreme

The Jules Verne Undersea Lodge was once a research laboratory off the coast of Key Largo, Florida. It is now a hotel. More than 10,000 guests have stayed there.

PRESSURE CHANGE

The pressure around Aquarius is 2.5 times higher than at sea level. The air inside the cabins is kept at the same pressure as the water. Divers can go in and out without a problem. However, to return to the surface, divers must sit in a **decompression chamber** for 17 hours. The pressure inside is reduced slowly to match that of sea level.

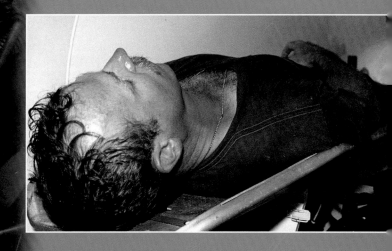

▲ *A diver rests in a decompression chamber.*

DRILL

The bottom of an ocean is also an important source of **petroleum**. Drilling platforms allow workers to live far out at sea. They can be anchored to the seabed, or float. They have huge drills that bore into the ocean floor to find oil and gas.

▼ *There are several methods of getting at oil buried under the seabed. Floating platforms can be towed to new drilling sites. Sometimes, the drilling rig sits on the seabed. Each platform sinks several wells. The drills can twist and bend through rocks to reach the oil. Huge tanker ships collect the oil and take it to shore.*

Vital Statistics

✳ The Deep Sea Drilling Project is a scientific program for collecting samples of rocks from the seabed.

✳ The program has found thick layers of salt under the ocean floor.

✳ It has also found proof that the continents and seabed are moving.

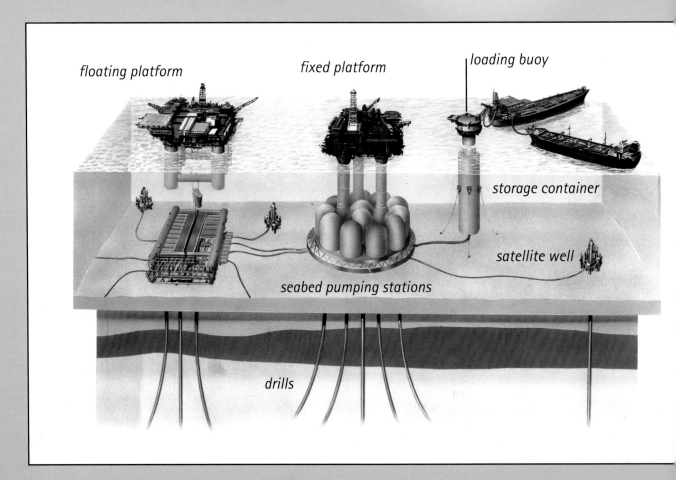

floating platform

fixed platform

loading buoy

storage container

satellite well

seabed pumping stations

drills

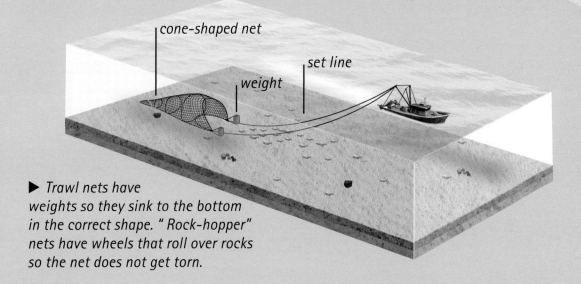

cone-shaped net

set line

weight

▶ Trawl nets have weights so they sink to the bottom in the correct shape. " Rock-hopper" nets have wheels that roll over rocks so the net does not get torn.

HARVESTING THE SEA

The sea has been a good source of food. Fish such as sardine, tuna, and mackerel are caught near the surface. However, cod, flounder, crabs, and shrimps are found near the bottom. Fishing boats are trawling deeper than ever to catch fish.

SCRAPE THE BED

Deep-sea trawlers drag huge, heavy nets along the bottom of the oceans. The trawl net can damage the seabed and kill animals, such as sharks, that are not wanted by the fishers.

CHANGING SHAPES

Earth's crust is made up of sections called plates. Rocky plates float on the liquid rocks deep inside the planet. The thin crust is seabed, while thicker parts form land. The plates are moving as new crust is formed in one place and melted away at another. As a result the oceans are gradually changing shape. The Red Sea (right) is growing. In 200 million years, it will be as wide as the Atlantic is today.

EXTREME FACTS

ON THE ROCKS

Corals (*below*) may look like colorful plants but they are actually animals related to jellyfish. Each tiny coral anchors itself to a rock and filters food from the water. They also have algae living inside them, which supply the coral with food. Corals live in huge colonies called reefs.

LITTLE AND LARGE

The anglerfish has a very strange mating system. Adult males are only a fraction of the size of the females, and they have no stomach—all they want to do is mate. Once a male finds a mate, he bites her very hard. His mouth becomes fused to her blood supply. He lives like a **parasite** on the female's back. The male gradually stops looking like a fish, and soon all that is left is his sex organs. These wait for the female to lay eggs and then release sperm. A two-foot (61 cm) female may have several "mates" living on her.

HUGE FISH

Some reports of sea monsters (*left*) may have actually been giant oarfishes, which grow to 50 feet (15 m) long.

TINY AND TOUGH

The bacterium *Pyrolobus fumarii* can survive in boiling seawater.

MIX IT UP

It takes 1,000 years for ocean water to circulate around Earth.

RED WATER

Dinoflagellates are tiny living things that float in seawater. In certain conditions, dinoflagellates bloom. They increase to huge numbers. The bloom turns the water red (*right*).

MONSTER VENT

A black smoker nicknamed Godzilla holds the record for growing the fastest. It grew to reach 165 feet (50 m) high. Then it fell down.

GLOSSARY

abyssal Describing a huge empty space

atmosphere The air surrounding Earth

bacteria Tiny living things

ballast Weights used in ships and subs

camouflage Coloring that blends in with surroundings

cells Tiny units used to make up a body

crust The outer rocky covering of our planet

decompression chamber A tank used to help people get used to different pressures

dense To have a lot of material squeezed into a small space

dissolved minerals Chemicals that are invisibly mixed into water

freshwater Water without salt in it

hydraulic Powered by pumped liquids

hydrothermal vents Cracks in the seabed that release hot water

invertebrate An animal without a backbone

magma Hot liquid rock under the ground

mammal A warm blooded animal that produces milk for its young

marine Of the ocean

methane The scientific name for natural gas used in stoves and heaters.

NASA The U.S. space agency

nitrogen The most common gas in the air

nutrients Useful chemicals in food

optical fibers Communication wires that carry signals as beams of light

oxygen A gas in the air used by living bodies to breathe

parasite An animal that lives on another

petroleum Oil and gas found in rocks

predators Hunting animals

pressure How much air or water pushes down on an object

pupils The holes in eyes that let in light

sea level The point from which the depth of an ocean is measured

vertebrates Animals with backbones

volcanic eruptions When magma bursts out of the surface of Earth

FURTHER RESOURCES

BOOKS

Deep, Deeper, Deepest: Animals That Go to Great Depths by Michael Dahl. Minneapolis, MN: Picture Window Books, 2006.

Deep Oceans by Wendy Pfeffer. New York, NY: Benchmark Books, 2003.

Sperm Whales and Other Deep-Water Life by Sally Morgan. Mankato, MN: QEB Publishing, 2009.

The Deep-Sea Floor by Sneed B. Collard. Watertown, MA: Charlesbridge Publishing, 2003.

WEBSITES

Discovery Channel: Titanic

dsc.discovery.com/convergence/titanic/titanic.html

National Geographic's Oceans page

science.nationalgeographic.com/science/earth
/surface-of-the-earth/oceans-underwater.html

NOAA Ocean Explorer

www.oceanexplorer.noaa.gov

Videos and Animations from Woods Hole Oceanographic Institute

www.whoi.edu/page.do?pid=8876

INDEX

Printed in the U.S.A. — BG